Princess Warrior: Lessons Learned from Zamora

Edited by Dr. Patricia Salahuddin
(Zamora's Grandmother)

BOOK POWER PUBLISHING

Princess Warrior: Lessons Learned from Zamora

Copyright ©2026 by Patricia Salahuddin

Published in the United States by Book Power Publishing, an imprint of Niyah Press, Detroit, Michigan.
www.bookpowerpublishing.com

Cover designed by Yasin Parris, Zamora's cousin

First Edition

PRINTED IN THE UNITED STATES OF AMERICA

Paperback ISBN: 978-1-964965-25-3
Hardcover ISBN: 978-1-964965-24-6
Ebook ISBN: 978-1-964965-23-9

In loving memory of Zamora Salahuddin
November 18, 2013 – June 27, 2024

Princess Warrior Zamora

Her legacy of love, courage, and joy lives on
in every heart she touched.

Contents

Introduction

In May of 2021, COVID-19 was in full force. No social gatherings were allowed, including religious ones. In our Muslim community, this meant we couldn't gather at the Masjid to perform our traditional Eid prayer, nor could we meet at the local park to celebrate the end of thirty days of fasting.

However, having a large family made it easy for us to pray together at my home. Following the prayer, we celebrated with a hearty breakfast: pancakes, eggs, shrimp and grits, and all the other favorite family dishes that filled the table.

Having been separated for so long due to COVID, the joy of simply being together filled the air. There were stories, laughter, teasing, and connection. I was busy clearing the counter, setting up the pancake griddle, and preparing the kitchen to receive the pots and bowls of food each family had brought.

My youngest son, Wali—Zamora's father—placed his bowl of fruit on the counter. As he removed the top from his mix of tropical fruits, he spoke in his usual academic tone:

"We got the results from the biopsy."

My hands stopped moving. I stood upright, tense, staring into his face, waiting to hear the words I desperately wanted to hear. The room went silent.

"It's cancer," he said.

Those were not the words I wanted. Not again—cancer.

"It's cancer." The same phrase I had heard years ago, when my husband and I sat listening to the doctor deliver his diagnosis. Now I was hearing it again—but this time, it was about my grandbaby. The youngest of my seventeen grandchildren. The youngest of the eight girls, Zamora.

Zahirah, the oldest grandchild, is also a girl. She affectionately calls Zamora "Little Z" and herself "Big Z."

I didn't want to hear this news—not on this day, not on any day. My prayer was that Wali would say it was benign. So I asked: "What kind?"

"Osteosarcoma," he replied.

"It developed in her right leg, just above the knee."

The name meant nothing to me. I took a deep breath and pushed out the question I really needed answered.

"Is it benign or malignant?"

"It's malignant," he responded gently, in his usual soft voice.

"She gets a port in two weeks and starts chemo in June."

I closed my eyes and tried to steady my breathing.

"She's only seven years old. How can that be?" I thought to myself.

I wanted to hold her, hug her, but COVID precautions kept her and her mother home for safety.

But where is the protection from cancer?

Zamora was still in elementary school. The thought of her having to endure chemotherapy at that age was heart-wrenching. I remembered what her grandfather went through after each session—vomiting, weight loss, no appetite, no energy.

Would Zamora have to suffer like that too? The very thought made me feel numb.

On this day of celebration, my heart was overwhelmed with pain. I longed to see her, to hear her voice—but I couldn't speak. My voice wasn't ready. I remained silent, deep in thought about the road ahead.

I had been down this rugged road before.

Though my hands kept working, my mind was stuck in one place: cancer.

And we had not had success with cancer.

How would Zamora respond to this reality? She was just a little girl. What would she think of this illness?

I was struggling with the news, and I'm an adult! How could she possibly handle it?

Then, I remembered the only source that truly calms the heart and lifts the burdens of sorrow: I turned to God in prayer. I reminded myself that Allah is in control, and He grants what He wills. I asked for ease, for guidance, and for the strength to accept whatever He had decreed. Slowly, the heaviness in my heart began to lift.

The next day, I spoke with Rovina, Zamora's mother. She was calm—and I needed that. She assured me that Zamora was doing well, and that her attitude was bright and positive.

Then she told me something that truly brought me peace. Zamora had said to her:

"Don't worry, Mommy. God takes care of babies. I will be alright." Those words revived me. I felt alive again. I needed to hear that Zamora was in good spirits—not depressed or afraid. She wasn't sorrowful. She wasn't broken.

She was a warrior.

She didn't crumble. She fought.

Over the next three years, as I watched this remarkable child face surgeries, chemotherapy, and the amputation of her leg with unwavering courage and joy, I realized that Zamora wasn't just fighting cancer—she was teaching all of us how to live.

After Zamora returned to her Creator on June 27, 2024, I knew her lessons were too precious to lose. This book began as my attempt to preserve her memory, but it became something much greater.

When I reached out to family, friends, teachers, and caregivers, asking them to share how Zamora had touched their lives, the response overwhelmed me. Story after story poured in, each revealing the profound impact one small girl had made simply by being herself.

Princess Warrior Zamora: Lessons Learned is our collective love letter to an extraordinary child who redefined strength, showed us the power of optimism, and proved that the smallest souls often leave the biggest footprints on our hearts. These tributes—from her favorite cousin to her school nurse, from her best friend to her doctors—capture the essence of a girl who chose joy every single day, even when facing the unthinkable.

Zamora lived only ten years, but in that brief time, she taught us lessons that will last a lifetime. Through these pages, her light continues to shine, reminding us all to live fully, love deeply, and face each day with the fearless spirit of a true warrior princess.

Dr. Patricia Salahuddin
Zamora's Grandmother

The Journey: Timeline

Before Ringing the Bell: Chemotherapy Experience

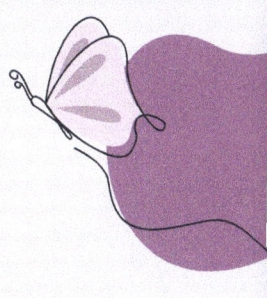

2021

- May 18 — Was diagnosed with Osteosarcoma.

- June 1 — Less than two weeks after her diagnosis, Zamora had surgery to insert a port in her chest for chemotherapy.

- June 2 — She began her first chemo treatment.

- August — After two months, it was determined the initial chemo was ineffective; the tumor had grown and passed her fibula growth plates.

- A new chemo cocktail was introduced. Miraculously, the tumor began to retreat after just one session.

- Over the course of four chemo treatments, numerous scans, X-rays, and MRIs were performed to monitor the tumor and design a custom surgical implant.

- December 10 — Zamora underwent surgery to implant the custom device. She was excited to move forward. Thanks to excellent pain management and a nerve blocker, she never complained of pain. The very next day, she was walking again. After six days in the hospital, we went home.

2022

- January 3 — After three weeks at home, she resumed her 5th chemo session.

- August — Zamora received a new implant in her leg.

- November — The Make-A-Wish Foundation granted Zamora a dream trip to her favorite theme parks: Disney, Universal, and SeaWorld.

2023

- February — Surgery was performed to extend her implant and help equalize her legs.

- March — Through the Jorge Mason Foundation, our entire family received an all-expense-paid trip to Cancun.

- April — The surgical entry point for her leg extension did not heal properly, requiring a revision surgery to replace part of the implant.

- June–July — Nodules were discovered on her lungs along with a large mass on her right leg.

- July — The nodules were surgically removed.

● August — Her right leg was amputated. Incredibly, just one week later, Zamora was ready and excited for the first day of school.

● October — She underwent surgery to remove small nodules located between her lungs and diaphragm.

2024

● April — A routine scan revealed more nodules.

● May 8 — An exploratory surgery was performed to identify and remove tumors. Sadly, the cancer had spread extensively. There was nothing more the doctors could do.

● June 27 — No more surgeries. No more chemo.
On this day, our beloved Warrior Princess, Zamora, returned to her Creator.

Tributes

Rovina Salahuddin

A Mother's Tribute to My Baby Girl, Zamora

Zamora's Mother

From the very beginning, my daughter showed me what it meant to be strong. Zamora was born early, a tiny preemie who had to spend her first three months in the NICU. I remember sitting by her side every day, praying and nursing her, whispering again and again, "I just want my baby home." She was healthy in every way—her scores were strong—but her body just needed more time to grow. Those first months were hard, watching her so small, so still, when I had once given birth to a son who came out crying, moving, and full of energy. But Zamora was different. She was slow to grow, slow to move. And yet, from the very beginning, she was a fighter.

When she turned one, everything changed. Suddenly, she broke into her full personality. She started walking, playing, and moving with the other children. She blossomed. By preschool, she was outgoing, stylish, and loved to look nice.

Teachers at Clara Muhammad School admired her for being respectful, by-the-book, and eager to learn. She followed the rules, wanted to do things right, and carried herself with a maturity beyond her years

She had her quirks, too. As her mother, I noticed things others might not. She was highly intelligent but reserved in certain ways, sometimes holding back, sometimes unsure of how to join in with other children. But once she warmed up, she loved being part of the group. She adored cooking, dressing up, and laughing with her friends. She carried herself like a young lady, even when she was still so small.

Her bond with her big brother was special. She always wanted to be around him, even when he found her "annoying" like brothers do. They had their spats, but they needed each other. If she cooked, he would clean. If she wanted something, he would sneak to get it for her. He was her handler, her protector, even as he teased her. They were a team, even when they pretended not to be.

When Zamora was diagnosed with cancer, my world stopped for a moment. I had walked alongside my own mother through breast cancer, taking her to appointments, talking with doctors, and seeing the toll it took. I knew what this road would look like, and it sickened me to think of my baby facing it. That night, I stayed home with my Bible, praying through tears, asking God for strength.

When I told Zamora, she didn't break down the way I feared. She looked at me and said, "Mom, God doesn't let bad things happen to children." I will never forget that. Her faith was simple and pure. She believed God had her, and in many ways, that gave me strength to believe too.

From that day forward, I made a decision. I would not let my daughter's life be defined by cancer. We would not sit at home with sorrow. We would not drown in pity. We would live. Every weekend, we went out. After school, we went to events. I signed her up for painting classes, parties, and programs that gave her outlets beyond the hospital. Joe DiMaggio Hospital, Gilda's Club,

Even after surgery, she amazed everyone. I remember one outreach event just weeks later. There was Zamora, standing on one leg, jumping around with her friends, laughing like nothing had happened. People asked me, "Why aren't you hovering over her?" But I believed in giving her independence. I let her shine, because she was still Zamora—not just a patient.

She never let cancer take her joy. She was an honor roll student the entire time. She made friends, danced, laughed, and even traveled. We took her on her first cruise to the Bahamas, and we were so proud of the independence she had. She checked herself in and out of activities, managed her schedule, and carried herself like a young woman. Watching her live like that, even in the middle of treatment, filled me with pride.

Everyone wanted Zamora around them. Friends' mothers would call me directly, double-checking if Zamora was coming to the party or the event, because if she wasn't, their own children didn't want to go. That was the kind of magnetism she had. She lit up every space she walked into.

And she was unstoppable. I'll never forget the time she had to go to the ER in the morning. By afternoon, she insisted on still going to an event with her friends. Even with pain in her body, she looked at me and said, "Mama, can you take me? I'll be okay." And sure enough, she was there with her friends, laughing and present, not letting the illness steal her joy.

Zamora never sugarcoated the truth. One day she looked at me, calm and serious, and said, "Mommy, I think I'm done with chemo and surgeries. If there's no more, then the only thing left is death." My heart broke, but I also admired her strength. I told her, "Baby, only Allah knows when that time will come." She shrugged, accepted it, and then, in her way, moved on to the next moment—asking what was for dinner. That was my daughter. Honest. Courageous. Unafraid.

Through Zamora, I learned patience. I learned to slow down, to listen, to let go. She showed me strength I didn't know was possible. If it had been me, I don't know if I could have endured what she did with such grace. But Zamora never cried about her illness, never complained, never asked "why me." She just lived. She carried herself with dignity, with humor, and with faith.

I know people expect a certain kind of grief. Some look at me and wonder why I don't cry the way they think I should. But I feel peace because I know God was merciful. Zamora didn't suffer the way many fear. She lived with joy, and when her time came, I knew she had fulfilled her purpose. We are not meant to be here forever. We are here to serve a purpose. And my Zamora served hers—touching her classmates, her teachers, her doctors, her friends, and her family. She gave others strength, even as she carried her own burdens.

I thank Joe DiMaggio Hospital for their care and compassion, and I thank the many organizations that stepped into our lives to bring smiles to my daughter's face. They gave her laughter, friendship, and experiences that helped her feel whole. For that, I will always be grateful.

To Zamora

My sweet baby girl... I love you forever. You were my fighter, my joy, my teacher. You showed me patience, courage, and faith. You lived your life fully, even in the face of the hardest trials. Everyone who knew you loved you, and everyone wanted to be around you. I carry you in my heart every single day, and I am grateful for every moment we shared. Until we meet again, you will always be with me.

Wali Salahuddin

You Won The Race, Patiently Persevere

Zamora's Father

On May 18, 2021, our little Warrior Princess was diagnosed with osteosarcoma in her right leg, just above the knee. Over the course of her three-year journey, my daughter patiently persevered through countless needle pricks, numerous X-rays, CT scans, MRIs, and eight surgeries—including the eventual amputation of her right leg. Although the cancer overtook her body, it never touched her mind or her spirit. Until the very end, Zamora remained a happy, well-balanced 10-year-old who loved learning, playing, signing, dancing, and helping others. Osteosarcoma never defined her—it was simply a fact of her life.

A Daddy's Girl

From the very beginning, Zamora was bright eyed. She came early—nine weeks before we expected her—but her eyes were wide open, bright, alert, already taking in the world. From the start, she had this look of focus, like nothing was going to stop her.

Always in My Arms

I guess you could say Zamora was a daddy's girl. She got away with a lot, and I didn't mind. I was always carrying her—just like I did with all my kids—but with her, it was different. Whether we were walking from the parking lot to the doctor's office or just moving around the house, she was always negotiating and trying to make a deal with me—"Can you carry me?" Carrying her wasn't just about getting from one place to another; it was our time together, a way for me to hold her close and let her know I was always there. Even as she grew, she'd find a way to climb up and sit on top of me, just to be near. I remember one day I was completely exhausted, just lying down trying to rest. She came right over and climbed on top of me, settling herself in like she always did. She was ten by then, already living with one leg after the amputation, but that didn't change a thing.

Our "picnic"

We had our special moments. I remember there was one memory she always carried with her—what she called our "daddy-daughter picnic." I had kept a condo when we moved into a house.

One morning, I had to stop by, and she was with me. We picked up Panera breakfast, sat on the floor of the empty condo, and ate together. No furniture, just us on the carpet. For me, it was ordinary. For her, it was a picnic with her dad. She brought it up again and again, remembering it as a special moment. That was Zamora—she cherished the simple things.

She also loved little surprises from me. Once, after a checkup with her orthopedic surgeon, we were driving home on the highway. There was a long on-ramp, and I knew she liked the thrill of speed. So I pressed down, letting the car accelerate fast. She got that roller-coaster jolt and burst out, "I love you, Daddy!" It was so pure and spontaneous. She loved the excitement, and I loved giving it to her.

Navigating Her Illness

When Zamora got sick, my wife and I naturally split responsibilities. She managed the oncology side—the chemo, the treatments. I managed the surgical side. That meant most of the surgeon appointments, scans, and follow-ups were my time with Zamora.

Those appointments became "our thing." From the walk in the parking lot, to waiting in the office, to passing time with jokes, songs, and little dances, she made even the hospital fun. And always, there was a deal to be made: "Daddy, if you carry me, then I'll..."
She kept negotiating right through it all.

Her medical journey was tough and challenging, but it never felt burdensome. That was thanks, in part, to the compassionate care of Joe DiMaggio Children's Hospital and their incredible Child Life professionals, like Samantha Utter, along with their service partners: Gilda's Club South Florida, Freedom Waters, and N.I.C.K./Camp Boggy Creek.

Zamora looked forward to her visits—not just for the gifts, but for the joyful in-hospital activities like music therapy, yoga, art, and educational programs. She also delighted in the unique life experiences made possible by these organizations: tickets to the 2024 Stanley Cup Finals to see the Florida Panthers, Marlins Club Level games, Make-A-Wish experiences, Freedom Waters boat rides, Jorge Nation Foundation's Spring Break getaway, Disney on Ice, and much more. She was never overwhelmed by "being sick." In fact, she was relatively unfazed by her diagnosis—always eagerly anticipating the next adventure or camp.

When we first heard the diagnosis, my wife was overwhelmed. But Zamora looked at her calmly and said, "I'll be okay, Mommy." That was her spirit: even when she was the one suffering, she was the one doing the comforting.

When we learned she would need her leg amputated, she wasn't afraid. She joked, "So I'll be like a pirate?" And then, imagining herself with a robotic prosthetic, she laughed about being a "robotic pirate." That was Zamora—turning fear into fun, turning pain into play.

She wanted normalcy. I remember how badly she wanted to stay in school. During chemo, she had to be homeschooled for a time. But the moment she finished, she insisted, "I'm not going back to homeschool. I want to be with my friends." Even after a major surgery on a Thursday, she was back in school by Monday. She refused to miss life.

Her educational journey during this time was just as purposeful and inspiring. Thanks to the amazing administration, staff, teachers, and students of Nova Eisenhower Elementary (NEE), Zamora continued to thrive. She loved her school community—especially her dear friends Meliyah Daniels, Rachel Francois, Alisha and Shannon Rozier , to name a few. If she had major surgery on a Thursday, she was determined to recover in time to return to school by Monday. She was committed to learning, playing in the "Bad Lands," and reading her jokes on the morning announcements.

Her Strength and Her Legacy

Zamora didn't just fight for herself—she gave strength to others. At Gilda's Club, she became a leader. Children with cancer, children whose parents had cancer—everybody wanted to be around her. If she wasn't there, they didn't want to go. If she was there, they couldn't leave. She was asked to speak to other kids, to share her outlook. There was one 13-year-old girl who was fragile and closed off—until she met Zamora. My daughter brought her out of her shell.

Zamora was like a little Les Brown, lifting people, motivating them just by being herself. She also had a deep sense of fairness and insight. I remember her classmates were selling Girl Scout cookies. They were twins, one outgoing and one quieter. Zamora said, "Alisha gets everything. I want to buy from Shannon." She saw people for who they were and wanted everyone to feel seen.

And she never stopped living.

Over Memorial Day weekend, she went fishing with friends, flying down the path on her scooter so fast I had to switch to an electric bike to keep up. "Eat my dust!", she called out. She even went indoor rock climbing, scaling up 45 feet with one leg! Nothing could hold her back.

Her light touched so many people—from all walks of life. If you met her once, you'd remember her forever.

Patient Perseverance

Zamora was the embodiment of patient perseverance. In the Qur'an, Allah reminds us to "patiently persevere" through life's great challenges and tests. The Prophet Muhammad (peace and blessings be upon him) gave us the perfect example of this principle throughout his life.

Watching Zamora's brave fight against osteosarcoma reminded me of the strength and courage required to persevere with patience. It was a daily act of intentionality—to face adversity and never lose faith in Allah or His plan. From the very beginning, Zamora told Rovina that she would be okay. "God takes care of children," she said. She had no idea what lay ahead, and neither did we. But whatever came, Zamora met it with strength, courage, focus, and her signature sass. She did what had to be done—and then moved on with life.

Even in the midst of her own trials, she found ways to help other kids discover their own inner strength, inspiring them to meet their challenges head-on and move forward.

You Won the Race

Even on her last day, you wouldn't have known it was her last. Family and friends were visiting. She was laughing, drawing pictures on the whiteboard.

One drawing stands out. She sketched herself and her brother in a race. She drew herself ahead, nearing the finish line, with a big sun on the other side of the line. She gave herself angel wings. And in a speech bubble, she wrote, "I win."

That picture told me everything. She knew. She understood. She wasn't afraid. She was telling us that she had reached the goal before us. That she had already crossed the finish line. My father, before he passed in 2017, reminded me: "We're not here forever. We live for the hereafter. This life is just the race to get there." I shared this understanding with my children and Zamora knew that. She beat us to the finish line, and she finished strong.

To Zamora

My baby girl, I love you. I miss your laugh, your spunk, your way of making deals and acting like we all worked for you. You brought joy wherever you went, and you taught me what real strength looks like. You reminded me to live with faith, to laugh, to keep moving forward.You won your race. And I will always be proud to call you my daughter.

Zayd Salahuddin

Zamora's Brother

My sister was a positive, smart, strong willed young woman. She was young, but she acted and showed years of wisdom. Her story is a testament to her heart, soul and mindset. It demonstrates to us that it's really mind over matter. She inspires me continuously.

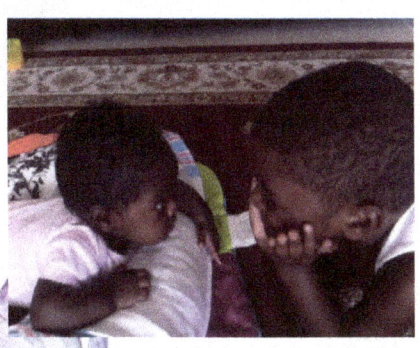

Zarinah Salahuddin

You Won't Break My Soul

Zamora's Sister

    The most profound lesson I learned from Zamora's life is that joy can exist even in the hardest circumstances. Despite battling a disease most people associate with adulthood, she never stopped being a kid. She still loved Disney princesses, the color pink, slime, pool water fights, pranking her brother, and hanging out with her friends. She sang, danced, hugged everyone she loved, and smiled through it all. At the same time, she carried a maturity far beyond her years—knowing her medications, monitoring her body, and speaking up when something didn't feel right.

    Being with Zamora brought out my own inner child. We painted our nails, baked whatever fun recipes she discovered on YouTube or Snapchat, played games, and watched cartoons. One Christmas she got a makeup kit from the hospital and insisted on being my makeup artist for the day—even though I hardly ever wear makeup!

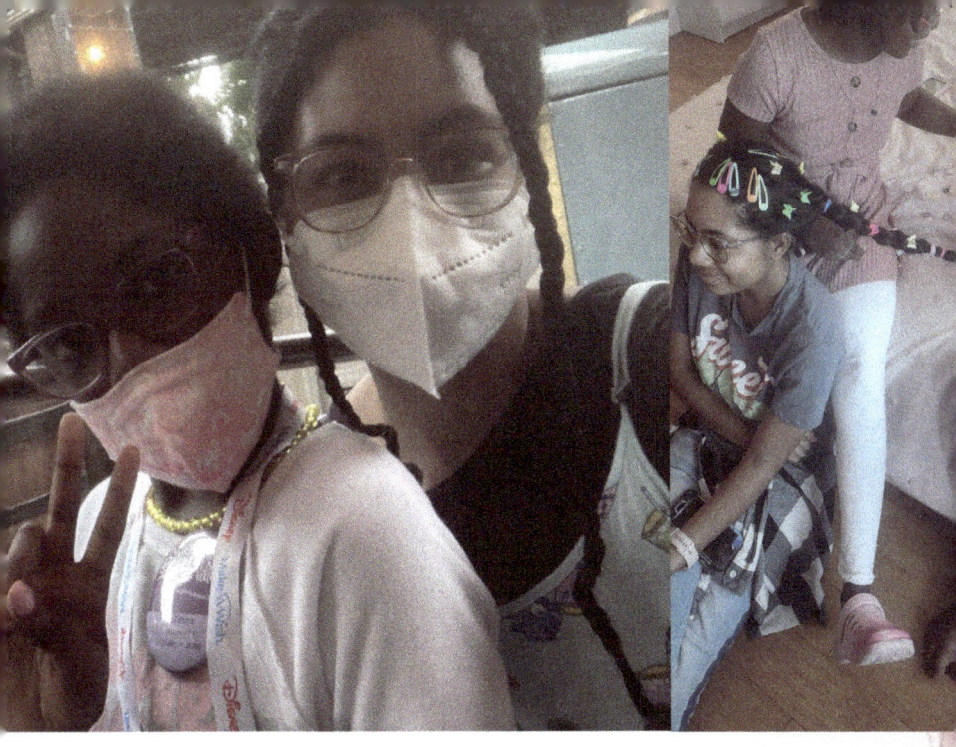

Our breaks together felt like long sleepovers, and for her 10th birthday we actually had one, where she and her best friend styled my hair (I still laugh at the photos).I never expected our fun to end so soon. I knew her cancer was aggressive, but I didn't think it would take her life. When I saw the video of her rock climbing to the top of a wall with one leg, it just reaffirmed what I already knew about my sister—she was determined, resilient, and unstoppable. Later, I came across a video I took a few years ago of Zamora dancing to Beyoncé's You Won't Break My Soul. Watching it again moved me deeply. She danced with so much freedom and power, and in that moment I could see her spirit shining through, declaring to the world that nothing could truly break her. That video still speaks to me whenever I need strength.

Reflecting on her life, I've taken on a mindset of joy, love, perseverance, and peace. Zamora reminds me to be mindful of the present and embrace the good in my life. She was assertive, bold, and knew how to go after what she wanted—and that inspires me every day.

Still, some memories I keep just for myself. She wasn't only a lesson, a light, or an inspiration—she was my sister. And there are special moments we shared that I'll always treasure privately in my heart, just between the two of us.

(The day I left for college. Zamora cried because she wanted to come help me move in. Our goodbyes often ended in tears, but I always promised her I'd be back soon.)

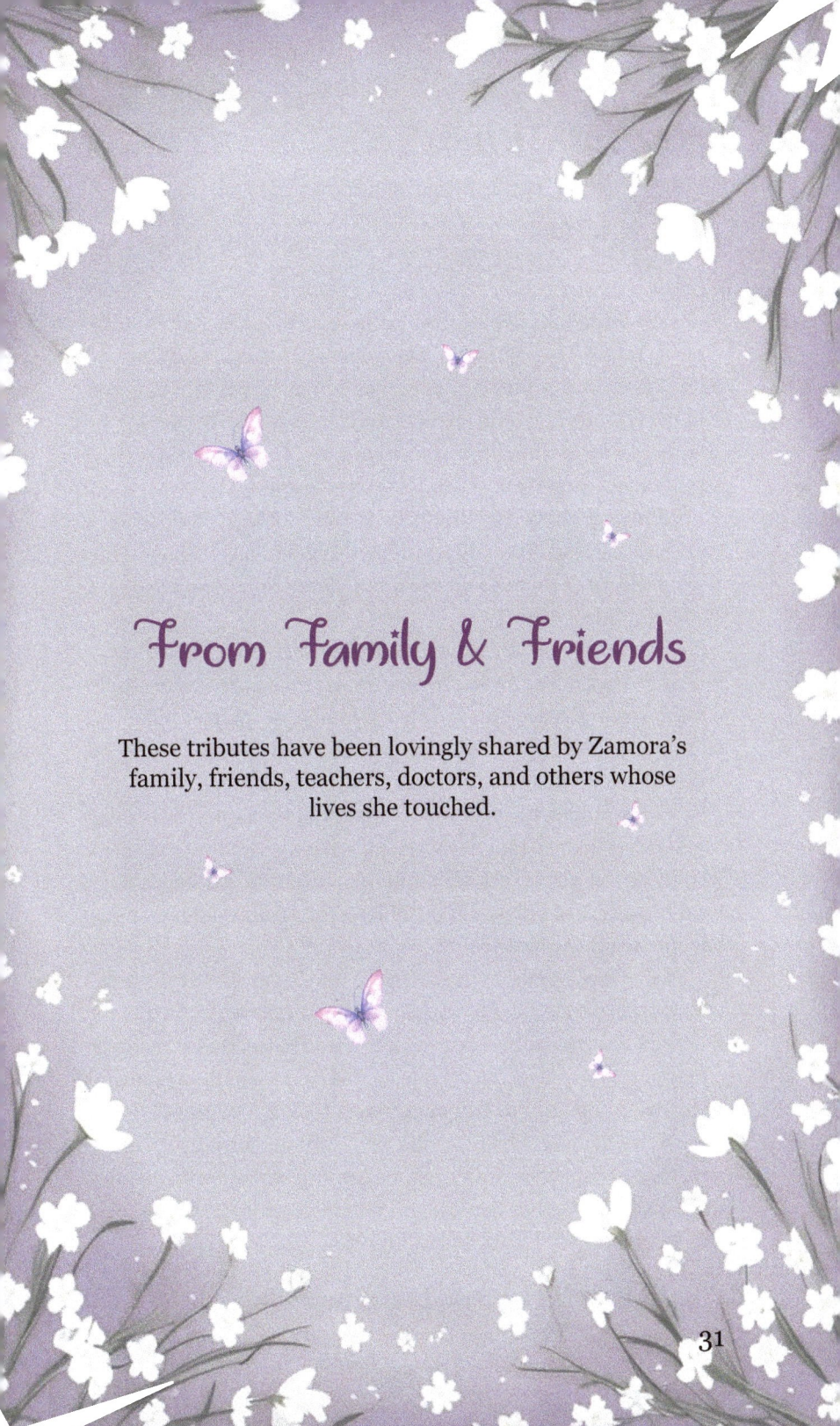

From Family & Friends

These tributes have been lovingly shared by Zamora's family, friends, teachers, doctors, and others whose lives she touched.

Stanfia Abbey

School Nurse, Eisenhower Elementary School

Love in Action

We often take life for granted and don't realize how good we have it. Enjoy every moment, cherish every second, and love hard. The first day I met Zamora was at her school. She had just had the amputation, and she was moving around like that leg was still there—never flinching or complaining. I was amazed by her strength and knew this girl had something special.

She once drew something for me that looked like Minnie ears, and she said, "I made you something because I thought of you." I still have them in my bookbag. Every time I look inside, I smile and think of her.

She lived—she didn't let the disease take over. She would talk about her adventures, sleepovers, and the parties she attended. She rock-climbed and rode some kind of scooter or bike. Nothing could stop her. She never wanted anyone to wheel her around in her wheelchair. She loved school.

She would come visit me asking for her pain meds (I could see in her little face that she wasn't having a good day), and she would beg me not to call her mom to pick her up. I thought it was funny—any other kid would be looking for an excuse to go home, but she was the opposite.

I'm a huge pasta lover, so I once told Zamora that for some reason, every time I heard the song "That's Amore" by Dean Martin, I thought of her. But my heart would feel this heaviness of happiness and light, and I'd hear: **"When your heart starts to shine, well it's no big surprise—IT'S ZAMORA!"**

She will always be remembered. Even my husband, who never got to meet her, thinks about Zamora whenever he hears that song. Thank you, Zamora, for shining your bright light on me. You are missed—but never forgotten.

Khalilah Abdullah

Family Friend

A Poetic Commemoration

There she is, Asalah, with firmness of step and

purpose,

Adorned with Latifah, showing kindness and grace.

She walks with 'Azima, braveness and resoluteness

around her heart revolve.

When faced with amputation, her only reply was

Ismail's: "Do as you are commanded."

Walk on Zamora to that eternal Firdous.

There, Al-Wadud awaits you with the embrace from

Al-Quddus.

Corrlette Asad

Community Auntie, Family Friend

Our Community Angel

Zamora was a gem. Her ever-present smile lit up the room as she greeted you with an intentionally warm hug.
I vividly remember our last hug.
Through all her health challenges, she exhibited the epitome of strength and determination. Zamora was a reminder to us all that in times of adversity, we must patiently persevere.
Zamora felt like she belonged to all of us—she was our sweet community angel.

As I continue to navigate through this life, I will forever cherish Zamora's spirit as a reminder that:

"Indeed, we belong to Allah, and indeed, to Him we shall return."

(Inna Lillahi wa inna ilayhi raji'un)

Fatima Bahmad

Family Friend

Life is Sacred

At just 10 years old, she carried a weight that would break most adults—yet she faced it with bravery, patience, sweetness, and a light that never dimmed, even as her body grew tired.
Her life taught me that every moment matters. Small kindnesses—a smile, a hug, a word of encouragement—can leave a permanent mark. She reminded me that life is short, unpredictable, and never promised, but also deeply sacred.

Since Zamora's passing, I've felt an urgency to be more present, to stop sweating the small stuff, to show up more fully for the people I love—and to speak words of love often.

Zamora didn't just fight cancer—she taught us how to live, how to love, and how to be grateful, even in the hardest moments. Her legacy is not one of tragedy, but of immeasurable grace.

It's hard to choose just one moment of strength, because Zamora's entire journey was a portrait of strength.
But one moment that deeply moved me was when—despite struggling to breathe and being in pain—Zamora still managed to smile at visitors.

Zamora showed me that true courage is choosing love over fear, peace over panic, and hope over despair—no matter what life looks like. I carry that with me every day.
I share Zamora's story with my students all the time. Because it's not just a story—it's a lesson for life.
When they say, "I can't," or when something feels too hard, I tell them about a little girl who had every reason to stop trying—but never did.

Zamora lost a leg to cancer. She needed a walker to move. Her body was in pain. Her lungs were tired. **And still... she climbed a rock-climbing wall.** I saw it in a picture her mom shared with me.

Ricardo Boyce

Great Uncle Ricky

I Finally Got My Hug

And it was not easy—I had to work hard for it. In the spring of 2017, during my stay in Miami helping my sister-in-law care for my beloved brother Khalid (Roddy), Zamora began stepping into my heart. She was about 5 years old then, vibrant and full of energy, with the most beautiful and loving smile. But for some reason, she would not give me, Uncle Ricky, a hug.

Every time she came over with her parents to visit her grandpa while I was there, I couldn't get a hug from that sweet, beautiful little pumpkin. She would run away laughing and teasing me every time I tried. I've been blessed with so many wonderful nieces and grandchildren, and it was never a problem getting their affection—but with Zamora, I had to earn it. She was playing hard to get, or so I thought.

It wasn't until a few months later, in December of that same year during a mini family reunion at Bashir's home in California, that Zamora and I finally bonded. But even then, the rejection continued, and I still had to work for it. After a few playful chases, I decided to try things my way. I pulled out the old reverse psychology trick—whenever she came near to tease me, I pretended to ignore her. And wouldn't you know—it worked!

Now, maybe her parents had convinced her to finally give her Uncle Ricky a hug, or maybe she just decided on her own. Either way, it worked—and I've got the pictures to prove it! That day, Zamora—my little pumpkin, that amazing, beautiful, sweet little girl—carved out a special place in her Uncle Ricky's heart.

She clung to me, having fun and showering me with hugs all day long. We were inseparable. It felt like she was making up for all the times she'd run away before, and she hugged me so much my granddaughters got a little jealous—they wanted in on the hugging party too!

That's how my beautiful little angel Zamora touched me, and why she will forever live in her Uncle Ricky's heart.

Melissa Boyce

Great Aunt

Extraordinary

"Our ability to handle life's challenges is a measure of our strength of character." — Les Brown

    I never had the privilege of knowing Zamora personally, but through countless photographs, I was fortunate to witness her spirit. That spirit inspired me.

    From her smile, one would never guess the battle she was fighting. Despite her youth, she embodied resilience—holding onto hope and positivity when many adults might have given up. She was truly an angel.

    I can think of many adjectives to describe her character, but the first is EXTRAORDINARY.

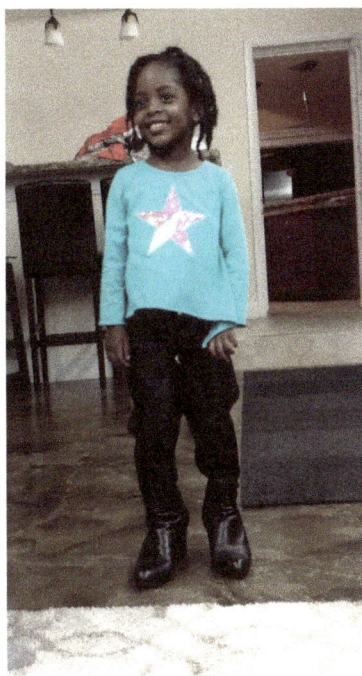

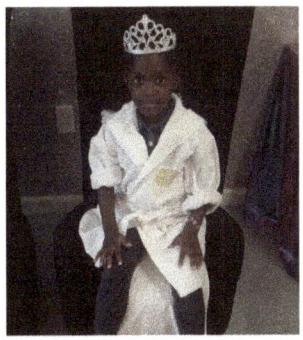

Zahirah Calloway

Cousin

The Brightest Light

Zamora was a testament to resilience. She faced every hurdle with a smile and never let anything keep her down. Even in her most difficult moments, she remained the brightest light. As someone who often struggles to see the positive, I now look to her life and memory as a reminder that we must hold on to optimism, no matter the circumstances.

I remember once taking Zamora and her siblings out for ice cream shortly after her leg was amputated. I braced myself for a heavy, solemn atmosphere when I entered the house. But the moment I stepped inside, I was met with deep, heartfelt laughter. My spirit immediately settled. It brought me so much joy to see her adjusting so quickly—and to see the light in her parents' eyes as they watched her.

Zamora was always smiling and giving hugs. She shared the love in her heart so freely with everyone around her. She was a beautiful child, inside and out. Every person who met her spoke highly of her generous spirit and hardworking nature.

Mubarak Calloway

Cousin

Glass Half Full

Life is all about perspective—and your ability to see things as "a glass half full." That is the most profound lesson I learned from Zamora.

When she went to the hospital to have her leg amputated, I was heartbroken. I kept thinking of all the ways it would impact her life. But the next time I saw her, she had the biggest smile on her face—almost like it didn't affect her at all.

I always felt loved in Zamora's presence. No matter how long it had been since I'd last seen her, she was always so happy to see me—so excited to play with me and the rest of our cousins.

It seemed like she never had a bad day when she was around family.

She left with me her outlook on life—the positivity and light she carried into every room. I plan to do my best to live my life to its fullest potential. To be present in every moment. To show up and support my family when called upon. And most of all, to be a "glass half full" kind of person.

Brooke Crawford

Zamora's Surgeon

Zamora loved to braid my hair. It's such a simple, normal thing for a young girl, but it was my favorite, striking memory of my visits with her. Because Zamora was in pain for a lot of the time I knew her. We met when her initial implant in her leg was loose, preventing her from walking or weight bearing. I diagnosed her recurrence at the time we were surgically fixing the loose implant, one of the worst moments in my career. But no matter how dire, no matter how much pain, Zamora would braid my hair. On one of her visits, I already had my hair in a French braid, for which she teasingly reprimanded me, and since then I made it a point to have my hair down for Zamora.

I have rarely met anyone, child or adult, who lived in the moment the way Zamora did. Her wonderful parents, Rovina and Wali, balanced her difficult diagnosis with all that entails with her also just needing to be a kid beautifully. Doctors' appointments were scheduled so she could get back to school, which she hated to miss. Rovina shared with me that Zamora had long before told her that she was ok with an amputation given how much trouble her post-tumor leg was giving her. Remembering that conversation really makes me smile because Zamora was not one to be slowed down, and if that meant a bad leg needed to go, she was all for it. So when we decided, after she continued to have significant pain in her leg, to amputate, she was so happy to show me how she was walking with her prosthesis she sent me videos of herself doing just that.

The morning after her amputation, Rovina shared with me that Zamora was doing great, moving around and feeling well, while the rest of us were adjusting to the loss of her leg at the hip. I operated on Zamora four times, and the way she was able to charm an entire operating room with her request for music and the way she would sing along - this was a child who truly was fearless.

My entire team, including myself, my scheduler, my nurse practitioner and other faculty who met Zamora absolutely fell in love with this girl. After her amputation, my scheduler found the biggest, pinkest teddy bear and we gave it to Zamora at her amputation post-operative visit. We anticipated her visits happily, because no matter how difficult of a day any of us was having, Zamora brightened it exponentially. More than that, when you meet with someone like Zamora, whose days are filled with dealing with cancer but she's focused on school and braiding hair, the miniscule annoyances and frustrations of daily life are revealed for the inconsequential distractions that they are. Here was a child who was fighting for her life, so what are we upset over?

My lessons from Zamora, which I hopefully illustrated somewhat here, are these:
1. The here and now are filled with delights - focus on those.
2. Deadweight is deadweight, even if you're attached to it - better to cut it off and get moving again.
3. Don't waste time fearing things you have no control over.
4. Be the person, moment, smile that lights up someone else's day.

I was so privileged to get to know Zamora and her parents; the endless capacity for love that we have was illustrated to me so clearly from all of them, and I will forever be grateful.

With love,
Brooke Crawford

Meliyah Daniels

Classmate and Best Friend

Yes, You Can!

I think the greatest lesson Zamora taught me is to always try my best and not say "I can't" before I even try. One time during lunch, I was really nervous about our end-of-year math test. I told Zamora I thought it was going to be way too hard and that I would probably only get a level two. But she looked at me and said, "You are going to do great." She believed in me, and because of that, I believed in myself. In the end, I passed and got a level three! That moment showed me how important it is to try and not give up, even when things feel scary.

Zamora had a really special way of making people feel happy and loved. One memory I'll always treasure is when we both bought the same comic book at the book fair called Frizzy. We were so excited and couldn't stop talking about it! We shared our favorite parts and our favorite characters, and it felt like we had our own little book club. That book brought us even closer and gave us so many fun memories.

Zamora made the little things feel big and special. Because of her, I try to be kinder and make people feel included—just like she always did for me.

Sylvia Daniels

Meliyah's Mom

Fearless

I first met Zamora and her mom on the first day of 3rd grade during open house. She and my daughter, Meliyah, just happened to sit next to each other—and from that moment on, it was like fate. They became instant friends, and as time went on, their bond only grew stronger. I stayed in touch with Zamora's mom, Rovina, especially after she mentioned Zamora would need to miss some school for surgery. We kept in contact in case classroom updates were needed, but more than that, our families became connected in a more meaningful way.

One memory that will forever stay with me happened just a week or two before Zamora's leg was scheduled to be amputated. She came over for a sleepover with Meliyah, and I remember being a little concerned—our house has two stories, and I worried she might struggle or be afraid to go up and down the stairs. But the moment Rovina left, Zamora and Meliyah were running up and down those stairs like it was nothing. At one point, Zamora turned to me with this playful, determined look and said, "I can't wait for this leg to be gone." It wasn't sadness—it was like she was saying, I'm going to make the most of every minute I have before it's gone. The strength and courage she carried, especially at such a young age, was something I had never witnessed before. She was fearless, full of light, and she made the decision—every single day—not to let her circumstances define her.

What struck me most about Zamora over time was her consistent joy. I knew she had cancer, and I was always hopeful that her treatments would lead to remission. And every time the cancer came back, she faced it with the same grace and strength. She never complained to my daughter. She wanted to go to school, be with her friends, and live life on her terms. That quiet independence and resilience taught me so much. She didn't want to be treated differently, and that was something I deeply admired.

The most profound lesson I learned from Zamora is that true strength doesn't always look like fighting loudly—it can be found in choosing joy, showing up fully, and holding onto hope even when life is unfair. Zamora's spirit left a permanent imprint on my heart. Her life, her courage, and her friendship with my daughter changed me forever. I try to live with more grace, more gratitude, and more perspective—because of her.

Olyvia Daniels

Meliyah's Sister

Unstoppable

One of my favorite memories with Zamora was when we went ice skating at the Panthers training rink. It was me, Zamora, her brother, and my sister—we were there with a childhood cancer group, and they gave us these big purple sweaters before letting us loose on the ice.

At first, I was low-key nervous. I kept thinking, how is Zamora going to skate? Is she going to be okay out there? But nope—she completely shocked me. She got out on the ice and was flying. Like, literally zooming past everyone. She was way faster than her brother, my sister, and even me. I couldn't believe it.

That day just showed how tough and amazing she really was. She didn't let anything stop her. She skated like a pro and had the best time—laughing and messing around like nothing else mattered. When I think of Zamora—her smile, her energy, her whole vibe—that day on the ice is what I always think of. She was seriously unstoppable.

Melvin Daniels

Meliyah's Dad

Resilience

—

One day, I was picking up my daughter, Meliyah, from Zamora's house after a sleepover. Zamora, Meliyah, and everyone were outside. Zamora was on the sidewalk, riding her bike. She had one leg—but you'd never guess it. She was riding like she had two—smooth, steady, and keeping up with her mom and dad like it was nothing.

I just stood there for a moment, taking it all in. She wasn't asking for help, and she wasn't struggling. She was just doing her thing, having fun, and fully in the moment. That really stuck with me. It showed the kind of strength and spirit she had, never letting anything hold her back.

Zamora was fearless. Seeing her that day reminded me what true resilience looks like. It's a memory I'll always carry with me.

Keyno Davis

Family Friend

Wise Beyond Her Years

Zamora was truly a Warrior Princess!

I never met her in person, but I spoke with her numerous times on the phone—and she was truly wise beyond her years. She was always respectful, but had a way of speaking that made you forget how young she was. Even after her diagnosis, she remained in high spirits; her personality never changed.

One thing that many of my family members who knew her have said is that she lived her life without self-pity. In the same situation, even some adults would crumble—but Zamora was strong. The message she unknowingly left with us is this: *Live every moment of your life to the fullest, regardless of the obstacles you may face.*

Raphinette McMorris Dunbar

Great Aunt

The Light of Love

The greatest lesson I learned was to make myself necessary for family. I need my family, and they need me. I'm so glad I was able to visit last June in 2024, before Zamora transitioned. Her presence was powerful—her vision was loud and beautiful. I will never forget her and her eyes. She shines like a light in my heart, and that light will shine forever. I think about her almost every day. I use her as an example in my life. Love was all around her, and it just rubbed off on everybody.

One moment of strength I'll never forget was when she held my hand for about an hour as we walked down St. John's Avenue in Riverside, Jacksonville, Florida, with her brother. Zayd was on my right side, holding my right hand, and Zamora was on my left. I enjoyed them both. It was such a loving moment—I didn't realize how close and connected we were until we walked into a candle shop and almost knocked over some of the beautifully scented candles. We hadn't even noticed them—we were so emotionally connected, so wrapped up in each other. I felt the warmth from her hands, and it was something I truly enjoyed and cherished. Then the store owner gently reminded us to be careful with the candles and glassware.

Zamora was love in action. When we were in Miami last summer (2024), we went to visit her. I could tell she wasn't feeling well, but despite how bad she may have felt, she still showed so much love to me. She got up and made egg salad sandwiches for us—and they were delicious. In that moment, I could see just how much love she had in her heart to give. I tried my best to receive it fully, because I truly appreciated it.

She was a wise warrior—yes, she was a warrior—but to me, she is my angel first. Being around her made my heart feel lighter. It gave me a reality check: to be thankful for what I can control, and to pray about what I cannot. Watching Zamora scoot around the kitchen with one leg was unbelievable. It gave me a whole new appreciation for her. And she did it with such flair—you would've thought she was about to perform a ballet. It was excellent.

There is so much she accomplished in her short life—it made her seem as if she had lived a hundred years. She taught us all so much. Anyone who ever experienced Zamora knows she experienced a great deal. Her legacy is enormous—so full of meaning and love, you can never get enough of her.
My tribute to her: keep shining in heaven, and those beautiful eyes will never be forgotten. Love you forever.

Tina Gilbert

Cousin

Love Never Ends

Though your time with us was far too short, your light shone with a warmth and joy that touched every heart you encountered.

You had a gentleness beyond your years—a quiet strength that reminded us of the beauty in simple moments.
In your laughter, we heard hope. In your courage, we saw grace. Your journey, though brief, has taught us that life is not measured by length, but by the love we give and the lives we touch.

Though we ache with your absence, we hold tightly to the promise that God, in His infinite mercy, has welcomed you into a peace far greater than we can understand.

Dora Boyce Gilbert

Great Aunt

My Beloved Zamora

Your zest for life and adventurous spirit have inspired us all. Though your time on earth may seem short to us, in God's eyes, you fulfilled the very purpose for which you were created. I am endlessly grateful for the profound impact you've had on our lives—both near and far.

You gave us unwavering love, boundless courage, and a fierce determination that continues to uplift us.
Your memory will live on in our hearts forever.
Love you very much.

Kena Gordan

Family Friend

Indelible Strength

The greatest lesson I learned from Princess Zamora is her indelible strength and endless courage. Zamora possessed a blessed gift that calmed the heart in her embrace upon greeting. She made it easy not to focus on her difficulties and instead see her in her beautiful wholeness. May Allah (SWT) grant her Paradise!

I vividly remember the first time I saw her with her walker—how she put it aside and pulled herself across the prayer area floor at Masjid Al-Ansar. She refused help, keeping up with her friends with confidence and exuberance. I thought to myself how much stronger she was than her illness, and that if she could have that much energy, then surely, we could be everything else she needed.

Princess Warrior Zamora showed her love in the way she hugged and laid her head on me when she greeted me—it was purely genuine. And in return, I now offer that same genuine compassion to others.

Zamora's confidence to face her battles with courage and determination helped me face challenges and hard times with the strength of her "warrior" mentality. Her brief life, in and of itself, has been a blessing—and has changed how I move through and respond to major events in my own life.

I honor Princess Warrior Zamora's life and legacy by reflecting on her journey through the eyes of the family and friends who remain. Her proud and beautiful family are all reflections of who Zamora was—and why she is known as **"Princess Warrior Zamora."**

Sr. Rosa M. Hallbrook
Family Friend

Angel

Zamora was like an angel in the flesh. She gave me more faith, seeing how pleasant she was through all her pain; she remained in good spirits. That knowledge and strength can be learned from the actions of a baby! Allah (God) has loaned all of us to each other, but we never know for how long. For that reason, we should treat each other with love and kindness while we are here together.

I consider Zamora my goddaughter because Zamora's maternal grandparents and I went to school together in South Miami, Florida. We have more in common: Zamora and my oldest granddaughter share the same birth month, November, though in a different date and year.

Dr. Dhakirah, Tahira, and Tariq Hamin

Family Friend

Never Left Out

Zamora taught us that optimism is a choice—and a powerful one. No matter what she faced, she carried a light and a smile that she refused to let anyone or any situation dim. The most profound lesson she taught us was to never let anything bring us down, no matter how hard life gets. She reminded us that even in the darkest moments, there is always a reason to hope, to smile, and to show others love.

One Eid, we were at the park, and most of the kids walked across the field—over a mile—to play on the swing set. Zamora was determined to go with them. They went up the hill, and so did she. I was so worried about her and kept checking in to make sure she was okay. She pointedly told me that she hates it when people "baby" her because she can do everything, and then proceeded to climb the steepest part of the hill. She even reassured me, saying she could just roll down while I carried her walker! In one last attempt, I showed her an alternate path that I needed to take because I was "too old"—and only then, she kindly agreed to switch her route.

She also taught us that each person can be whoever they want to be. No one has the right to define you or limit you. Zamora lived that truth boldly, and it gave all of us around her the courage to live more authentically, fully, and fearlessly.

What impacted us most was not just one moment, but the consistent strength Zamora displayed every time she came to the Masjid. Despite her physical challenges, she was determined to go upstairs and pray with everyone. Some weeks she enthusiastically hopped up the steps, and other weeks she scooted slowly and deliberately—but she always insisted on doing it herself. We watched from a safe distance, offering support only if she asked for it. She also insisted on praying while standing and making sujood during every salat. Week after week, she pushed her body to do what her heart and soul were committed to. That kind of devotion left a lasting imprint on all of us.

Zamora made people feel loved by making sure no one was left out. Whether it was a conversation or a special moment, she always included others. And she made sure she was included too—no matter the physical demands. Her way of loving was through presence, inclusion, and intentional kindness.
One of Tariq's favorite memories was talking with Zamora about Naruto, the anime series they both loved. It may seem like a small thing, but it created a bond between them that felt joyful and real. When they talked about their favorite characters and scenes, she would light up.

We intend to carry Zamora's legacy by choosing optimism every day, just like she did. She taught us that no matter what we are going through, we can still hold on to hope, joy, and light. Her ability to stay positive, even in the hardest moments, was more than inspiring—it was life-changing.

Now when we face challenges, we think of her. We remind ourselves to smile, keep going, and believe that better days are always ahead. That's how we honor her: by living with the same strength and light she gave so freely to everyone around her.

Dr. Afrah J. Hamin

Family Friend

Friends

Often, you meet someone whose personality touches your heart. For many, that someone was Zamora—the Warrior Princess. Her savvy ability to make others feel important radiated in every encounter. Zamora's kind-hearted and gentle manner shone through her attentive care for others.

The Hamin grandchildren—especially Inayah—would light up with excitement whenever Zamora was nearby. As soon as Inayah saw her, she would shout, "There's my friend! I have to play with her!" The two of them would pretend they were having a tea party. Zamora showed such care for Inayah, who was much younger. The younger Muslimah's shared a strong yet tender bond that felt completely natural.

The character traits that resonated with me most were Zamora's deep empathy and her intuitive awareness of how others were feeling.

As Zamora's health declined, I would often prod Tahira to keep a watchful eye on her. Although Zamora was fiercely independent, Tahira would gently offer to help her prepare for salat, stand, walk, or put on her shoes. And of course, the Warrior Princess would respond with, "I got it." Tahira would stand nearby—patient, present—giving her space to move on her own. Though their moments were often quiet, Tahira and Zamora showed up for each other with gentle hugs and warm smiles. Tahira instinctively recognized that Zamora's unspoken desire to lead was simply part of who she was—and honored it.

Zamora, Tahira, and Inayah shared an unspoken understanding of friendship. They could sense each other's feelings with just a glance. There was a special kinship between our Warrior Princess and the younger girls.

The life lesson I learned through my watchful eye is that Zamora deeply valued friendship. Even in her absence, her silence continues to teach us: to treat others with kindness, to slow down and have patience, and to lead with compassion.

Nia Jackson

Pre-K–1st Grade Teacher, Clara Muhammad School

Lead with Compassion

The most profound lesson I learned from Zamora was to always look for the good in people. No matter the situation, she carried a sense of light and hope that made others want to be better. Her presence reminded me that kindness is a strength—and that choosing love, especially in a world that doesn't always return it, is one of the most courageous acts a person can make. Zamora taught me to lead with compassion and to see potential even when others couldn't.

Every day with Zamora was a display of quiet strength, but one moment that stands out was when a classmate was struggling emotionally. Without hesitation, Zamora extended herself—not just with words, but with genuine concern and care. She sat with them, comforted them, and made sure they didn't feel alone. That kind of strength—the ability to put others first even when life is hard—is rare and unforgettable. It reminded me that true warriors aren't always loud; sometimes they're simply present.

Zamora showed love through joy. She had a beautiful spirit that lit up the room, and she loved to dance—it was her way of celebrating life and connecting with others. Her laughter, her smile, her willingness to share even the smallest moment with someone else made people feel seen and valued. As her teacher, I witnessed her kindness daily—she gave without expecting anything in return. Because of her, I try to be more intentional in how I show love to others, whether through a kind word, a warm smile, or simply being there.

Zamora's life was her message. She didn't need to speak loudly to make an impact. Her wisdom came through her actions—her consistency in treating people with respect, her courage to stand tall no matter what, and her joyful way of seeing beauty in everyone. She reminded me that no moment is too small to be meaningful, and that even in struggle, we can shine with grace.

I carry Zamora's legacy by trying to embody the same grace, resilience, and compassion that she showed every day. In my classroom, I speak her name when I see kindness. I think of her when students dance, when they laugh together, when they lift each other up. I pray that God blesses her with the highest level of Jannah—she truly deserves Paradise. Her life was a gift, and I am honored to have been a witness to her light.

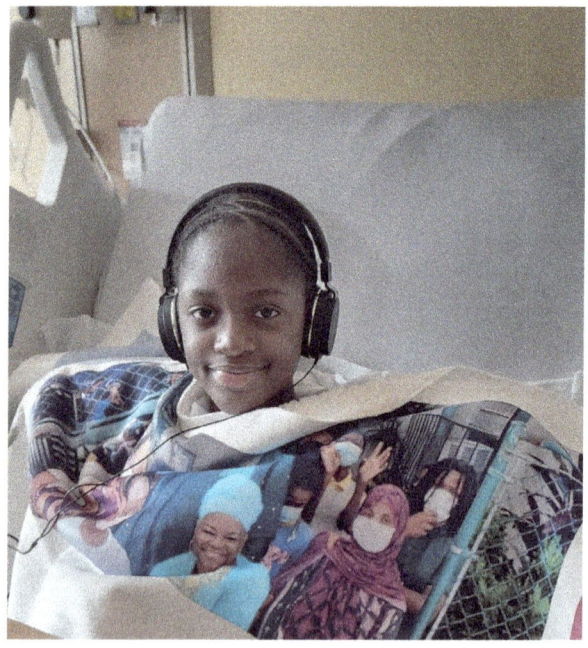

The Clara Mohammed School of Miami gifted Zamora
this beautiful blanket

Susan Lee

Camp Boggy Creek Director

Friendship

Zamora had a way of finding the light in any situation. Her impeccable comedic timing, ease in meeting new people, and kindness created a space where everyone felt welcome and included.

She was an artist—not only in the projects she created, but in the way she helped brighten any room she entered. There are many things about Zamora that showcased her strength, resilience, and courage. But the greatest lesson she taught was her love of school. Her determination to be part of the classroom, even on the hardest days, should serve as an example to us all: never take the simple things for granted— especially time.

Her ability to form new friendships and be a true friend to those around her was extraordinary. She had a remarkable way of connecting and listening to others. Her laughter was infectious and had a way of turning strangers into friends.

Zamora embraced life fully enjoying every moment, never taking the small things for granted, and living every minute to the fullest.

Zamora's family loved her from day one

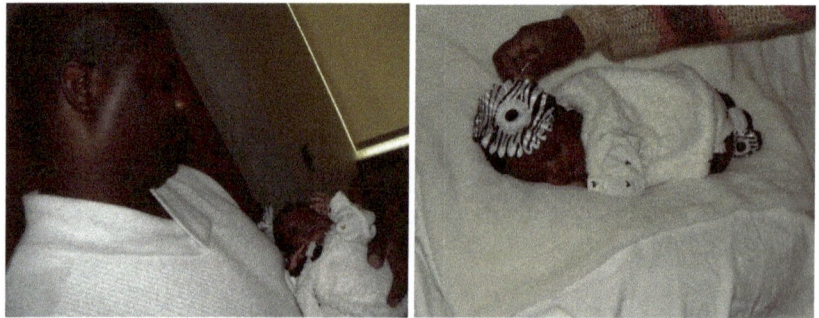

Early arrival and Stylish presence from the beginning

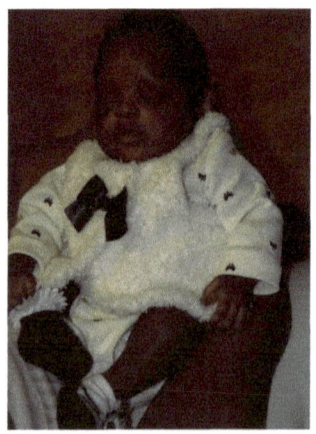

Michelle Martin

Teacher

My Best Friend, Zamora

    To my first best child-friend, whom I have known since she was in the womb of her mother.

My first encounter with Zamora was hearing her giggle in her mother's womb—telling me what a loving, wonderful, beautiful mother she had and how she couldn't wait to see her face. Zamora was a walking love bomb who exploded joy onto everyone she met. Wise beyond her years. A large glow of love embodied in a small little soul.

    Even though she has left this earthly realm, she will always hold a special place in my heart. The love we shared remains in my heart to this day—and forever more.

    Love never dies or fades.

    Rest in peace, my Princess. Love always, Best friend.

Alice Ollivierre

Artist Friend

The Artist Zamora

When Zamora was faced with yet another surgery, her response was, "Ok, let's just get it out." She never backed away from what was next on her journey. It made me think—there is nothing to fear when faced with a challenge. Stay strong in your faith and move forward to what's next.

What I loved most was the way Zamora smiled, leaned against me, and rubbed my arm. It was in that touch that I could feel her love.

We shared the joy of creating art. We had a day of paint pouring, and the messier it was, the better for Zamora. It was pure delight talking with her about paint colors and imagining what would happen as the colors moved and swirled across the canvas.

Zamora produced art with Alice Ollivierre, her family friend.

Qadir Parris

Cousin

Optimism is Zamora's Superpower

Zamora's life taught me to always find strength in the positive; her optimism was her superpower.
At the time, Zamora's knee was bothering her, but she didn't let that stop her from spending time with the ones she loved. That moment really showed how strong her heart was—and that I should have the same courage she did.

Zamora gifted me a bracelet a few years back that she made. I still have it to this day, as it's a sign of the love she had for her big cousin. That gift influenced me to value the time we have with people, because we never know how much time is left. She left me with the strength to always look on the bright side of things—because that's where you find strength in life.

Ray Parris

Uncle

Making Movez

Resilience was the lesson I learned from Zamora. She made me re-examine the essence of what it means to live in your purpose. Zamora always exhibited a spirit of happiness, and a powerful energy rooted in love and compassion for others.

Zamora had a special way of making people feel loved. She gave me the courage to be more understanding and more patient—especially in my work as an educator. I remember one particular day in the classroom when a student was having a tough time regulating his emotions. I thought about Zamora's strength, how she smiled through her pain, how she always placed others before herself. In that moment, I chose compassion over frustration. That's what Zamora taught me—how to lead with heart.

The insight I gained from knowing Zamora and watching her live through the challenges she faced is simple but profound: never give up, and keep a positive outlook on life, no matter the circumstance. Even in the middle of her own struggles, she made others feel seen and important. She carried herself with grace, as if her purpose was to care for others, even while carrying her own heavy load.

When someone leaves this world, they don't just leave behind memories—they leave behind power. Power in the lessons they taught. Power in the love they gave. Power in the dreams they dared to believe in.

To carry someone's legacy is not to live in their shadow—it's to walk in their light. It's to let their purpose live on through your actions, your words, your decisions.
I honor Zamora not by standing still in grief, but by moving forward with intention. By building what she started. By rising when it's hard. By becoming the echo of her impact—louder, stronger, unstoppable.

Her life story continues every time I choose courage, compassion, and truth. That's the power she left behind. And that's the power I will now carry.

Zamora demonstrated the power of making movez—and so will I.

Yasin Parris

Cousin

Just Do It

The most profound lesson I learned from Zamora's life is to always know what you want and never second-guess your decision.

One moment I look back on often is when I returned home to Miami for winter break and spent the evening with Zamora, her brother Zayd, my uncle, and auntie. Zamora decided she wanted to swim with me—even though it was cold. Zayd stayed out of the water, and honestly, I didn't want to swim either. But when Zamora made up her mind, that was it—she was going in. And because she wanted to do it, I felt compelled to join her.

Seeing how much she enjoyed herself, spending time with me despite the cold, made me realize how strong-willed and unbothered she could be when she wanted something. I really cherished that day. I got to grow closer to her and saw firsthand that when Zamora set her mind to something—she just did it.

Zamora was, without a doubt, a lovable person. She showed her love through playfulness and physical affection—teasing, playing, and always full of joy. I remember watching movies with her, and after each one, we'd end up tickling each other until someone gave up. It always ended with laughter and smiles.

Zamora also changed the way I look at life, especially when I'm in a bad headspace. I think about how she picked up hobbies like painting and knitting—creative ways she used to channel her energy into something physical and positive. That's something I still struggle with: finding healthy outlets for my energy. But seeing how she did it reminds me that it's possible—with practice and dedication.

I will continue to honor Zamora and carry forward the lessons she taught by standing by my decisions and following through with whatever I set out to accomplish. Her spirit reminds me: if you want to do something, just do it—even if the water's cold.

Quintera Salahuddin Parris

Aunt

Zamora—Princess Warrior

You could see in her eyes the look of a warrior—
determined, fierce, strong.
From the moment of her arrival, Zamora took the world by
storm.
Her thirst for learning, growing, and greatness was second
to none.
Age was truly just a number; it never stopped her from
surpassing her dreams or goals.
Rock-climbing, bike riding, swimming, bowling, skating,
baking, and dancing—she did it all!

One leg and all!
Zamora loved life—
Immensely. Intently.
Even through the most unbearable pain, unimaginable
setbacks, or life-changing limits,
she never wavered in her joy, in her purpose!
She loved without limits.

She hugged— **Long   Firm   Loud**

She lived and loved out loud!
Her love permeated the soul, bellowing, "You are loved!"
She relished every moment.
Nothing, no one
was taken for granted.
Savoring life until the very end,
basking in the love and light of family—
giving her final orders,
holding her cousin's hand,
sassing her brother,
kissing her mom and dad—
Grateful the fight has subsided and she is free to dance.

Zamora rock-climbing

Alia Pasha

Family Friend

Genuine Love

To stay positive—that's the lesson I learned from
Zamora. Every time she was faced with a new or recurring
challenge, she remained positive. She just kept going.
I remember watching her after her amputation, running
around with the children at Youth Islamic Studies with her
walker. She was having so much fun.

When I visited her in the hospital and Rovina said she
was having trouble breathing, I had brought some
cupcakes—and Zamora lit up. She never let on that she was
struggling. Her face was happy, and her spirit was high. When
I left that day, I felt good—not just about visiting, but because
of how strong that little girl truly was.

When Wali would bring Zamora to Jumu'ah, she would
leave his side and make her way to where the sisters were
sitting. She would pause, look around thoughtfully, and choose
where she wanted to sit. On the days she chose me, we hugged
tightly, and she gave me that unforgettable Zamora smile.

I remember one day at the Masjid, Zamora came to
school after one of her chemotherapy sessions. The treatment
had left her without any hair. Evidently, the students knew she
was coming—because as soon as she got out of the car, they
were waiting for her. They ran up shouting her name, their
faces glowing with happiness, greeting her with gentle hugs.
Of course, Zamora met them with her signature smile and
warm hugs. I was so impressed that not having hair didn't
seem to bother her in the least.

That moment helped me realize just how genuine the love was between Zamora and her classmates. It wasn't superficial—it was lovingly real. I was reassured and deeply moved. That day, I understood something important: courage and love have nothing to do with appearances. They have everything to do with honest, heartfelt care for one another. No one teased her. She was just happy to be among her classmates again—even if it was only for a visit.
I will continue to honor and carry forward the lessons and light that Zamora brought into my life—by remembering who she was, and all the things she did that were so honest and genuine.

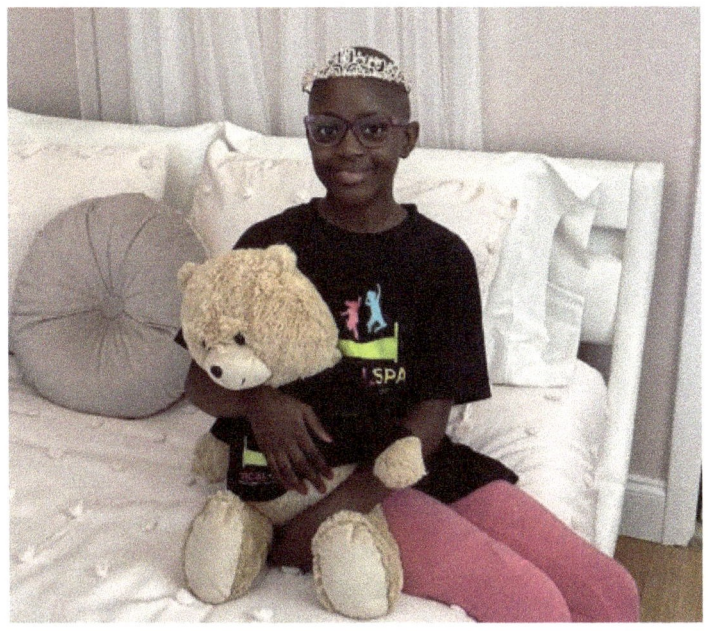

Fatima Ramzan

Exceptional Student Education Itinerant Teacher

Sassy

Zamora was a true force of love, happiness, strength, and resilience. She made a profound impact on every person fortunate enough to cross her path. I still remember the first time I met her—instantly, I felt a larger-than-life aura radiating from her. She was incredibly intelligent, insightful, and—my favorite quality of all—sassy! Nothing could stop her. Nothing.

Zamora taught me that it's okay to dance even when you don't feel like it, to sing even if your voice doesn't quite match the one on the radio, and—most importantly—to embrace and enjoy all the blessings around us, never taking a single moment for granted.
I absolutely adored Zamora. I think about her often and share her story with others, hoping her tenacity, joy, and zest for life will continue to inspire. She truly lived every minute of every day to the fullest.

Zamora, sweet princess—may your soul forever rest in peace, and may your light continue to shine brightly through the lives you've touched.

Forever Loved, Forever Missed.

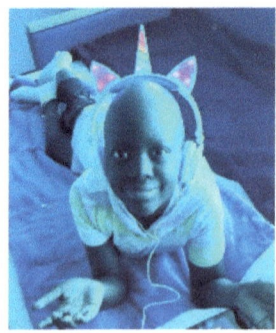

Nicole Rapp

Family Friend of Rovina

Gratitude and Kindness

Zamora's outlook on life truly serves as an inspiring reminder of the strength that positivity can bring—even in the toughest times. I use her positivity as a guide, reminding myself to reflect on my own life with gratitude, resilience, and absolute kindness. Even in photographs, her spirit shines with light and love.

Zamora's decision to stop treatments and embrace life was a profound display of strength and wisdom. That single choice highlighted the importance of cherishing each moment. Life is about experiences, connections, and joy—especially when faced with hard decisions.

She also showed true empowerment. By setting that boundary, Zamora took control of her narrative. It's a powerful reminder that we all have the right to make choices about our own lives and how we wish to live them.

I know it's said often, but it bears repeating—she was an inspiration. Her story encourages others to prioritize well-being and happiness, reminding us that it's okay to step back and evaluate what truly matters.

I carry her spirit in my heart. She's an incredible reminder to hold on to all the important things we so easily take for granted.

It's incredible how Zamora recognized the importance of seizing the moment and enjoying every experience. Her eagerness to return to school highlights a remarkably positive attitude—even in challenging times. Honestly, what kid ever wants to go to school?

The way she filled her heart with joy serves as a reminder for all of us to carry that same energy into our lives. I use this as a reminder to myself: when I exude joy, kindness, and love the way Zamora did, it helps soothe those around me—and I love giving people that peace.

A good question is: what wisdom did she not leave behind? She was wise beyond her years in how she viewed her life and made thoughtful decisions about her health. It reminds us how important it is to focus on what truly matters—and to take back control of our lives by choosing what brings us happiness.

Zamora's life was lived to its absolute fullest. The choices she faced were among the most difficult anyone could imagine. Yet, what stands out most is her deep love—for everyone and everything.

She gave people courage and hope. Her small soul made the biggest impact, and for that, she will always be remembered in a positive light.

She is a powerful reminder to cherish everything in front of you.

Kindness. Love. Courage.
The Princess Warrior Zamora. Her legacy lives on.

Alisha Rozier

Classmate and Friend

Kindness

Whenever Zamora was bullied by others, she continued to respond with kindness. No matter how she was treated, she remained gentle and caring toward everyone.

She came to school every day, even when she wasn't feeling well. That showed me that no matter what the situation is, I can push through and never give up. Zamora was always kind and thoughtful. From her, I learned the importance of showing kindness to others, no matter who they are.

Whenever we had a test, she would say encouraging things to me—simple but powerful words like, "Just do your best." Her support truly helped me.

Zamora's life taught me the value of being kind to others in every situation.

Shannon Rozier

Classmate and Friend

The Strongest Person I Have Ever Known

Zamora showed me what it means to be happy, even in hard times.
She never complained when people picked on her. From her, I learned not to let bullies get to me—and that silence can be strength.

She would go out of her way to do kind things for others. That taught me to appreciate people more and to give without expecting anything in return.

Even when she was tired or didn't feel well, she still did her schoolwork and homework. Watching her, I learned that you can keep going and do what you're supposed to do—even when you're going through things that no one else sees.
I keep the things she did in my heart, and I live by them like mottos for life.

I will cherish Zamora's love and friendship forever, and I will always remember her as the strongest person I have ever known.

Khalid A. Salahuddin III

Cousin

Perseverance, Adaptability, and Gratitude

The most profound lesson I learned from Zamora's life was witnessing someone so young embody the spirit of living every day to the fullest. With the time she had, Zamora lived in the moment—every single time I saw her. She always shared her excitement whenever she spent time with family. Her life reinforced something important in me: the importance of showing affection to my loved ones every time we're together.

After Zamora's leg amputation, the first time I saw her post-op stands out as a moment of true strength. Zamora hopped at full speed (which was still very fast and urgent!) straight into my arms for a hug. I watched her repeat this for all her cousins.

In my mind, I imagined the pain that must have accompanied that movement—but to Zamora, it was a victory. Being among her loved ones, getting another opportunity to share joy—that was her triumph.

Zamora's love, to me, was something I can only describe as pure—even angelic. Whenever she played, it was with the intention of sharing joy with others. Her love never wavered. She showed it through her energetic presence and infinite hugs. She always carried herself with a playful, spirited attitude that lifted those around her.

What Zamora's life taught me—on a deeper, spiritual level—is that Allah's mercy is truly infinite. I believe she understood that. Her steady focus on healing and moving forward, even through pain, showed me that life may be filled with strife and challenge, but we must always be diligent in appreciating the opportunities we're given—and remember to enjoy the time we are blessed with. Zamora's legacy, I believe, will live on through all of us—her family who loved her so dearly. She had a support system that cheered her on through every step of her journey. And I can say with confidence that all of us will be mindful of how we carry her memory.

To me, Perseverance, Adaptability, and Gratitude are the foundations of how I will remember Zamora. "My heart gets heavy when I think of her... but my resolve is to live on with her memory. She is an inspiration to me— my little cousin, Zamora."
The Baby of the Bunch. The Next Generation. We must not take things for granted. We must always give thanks for what we have.
We must find meaning in hardship. We must prioritize love and fun.

To me, these are the foundations of a fulfilling life: A life spent loving those around you—and being loved. A smile big enough to fill two rooms, and a heart bigger than the moon.
My little cousin Zamora, we love you.

Khalid A. Salahuddin, Jr.

Uncle

Gratitude and Resilience

The most profound lesson I learned from Zamora's life is the power of grace and positivity in the face of adversity. She never once complained during her battle with cancer—not even after losing her leg. Her attitude and outlook on life remained unchanged. She radiated positivity, and her light continues to shine even today. Witnessing her strength deeply impacted me. Because of her, I've made a conscious choice to stop complaining about the little things and to approach life with greater gratitude and resilience.

It was during a visit to the hospital, after Zamora had her leg amputated, that I witnessed her ultimate strength. To my surprise, she was full of life—almost as if she had been freed from a burden. She showed me the amputation with joy, while I was silently freaking out inside, overwhelmed by the situation. What moved me most was her spirit—just 36 hours after major surgery, she radiated strength and positivity. From that moment on, I realized Zamora didn't need anyone's pity. If you felt sorry for her, you were the one with the problem—not her.

Zamora had a beautiful way of making everyone feel loved. She always greeted people with a warm hug and a kind word, no matter the circumstance. What I loved most was that she never missed a chance to give—or receive—a hug from me. It was her way of making every moment count.

Her genuine kindness has inspired me to be more intentional in showing love and appreciation to others. One of the most powerful things Zamora ever showed me was that joy is a choice, even in the face of pain. She never let her circumstances define her spirit. Even after losing her leg, she smiled, laughed, and lived fully—reminding everyone around her that life is still beautiful, no matter what. That changed the way I see life. She taught me that strength isn't loud or showy—it's quiet, steady, and full of love.

Her wisdom continues to guide me: choose joy, be kind, and never waste a moment to make someone feel seen and loved.

I continue to honor Zamora by embracing life with the same joy, strength, and kindness she showed every day. I try to uplift others with a smile, a kind word, or a simple hug—just like she always did. Her light reminds me to live with gratitude, to face challenges with grace, and to never take the little moments for granted.

Carrying her spirit forward means being a source of love and positivity in the lives of those around me.

Mahasin Salahuddin

Aunt

A Blessing from Allah

Zamora was truly a blessing to our family from Allah. I can't say that she shaped my perspective, but she was a great reminder to remain positive despite the different tests and challenges you are faced with. On numerous occasions, I would hear about her health issues, and it would make me sad. But when I spoke to her, she was always so positive and upbeat—and it immediately made me feel happy. I would say to myself, "This is her life, and she is content with what Allah decreed for her. How can you be sad when she isn't sad?" Alhamdulillah!

Zamora lived a life of strength and resilience. Rahimahullah (May Allah have mercy on her). When I heard that her leg would be amputated, I asked how she felt or what her response was, and I was told she was very positive—like,

"If that's what they need to do, let's do it!" Very trusting and optimistic. Zamora was very loving and always greeted us with smiles and hugs. She always wanted to bake something to share with the family.

I make du'a (prayer) that Allah makes her grave spacious and blesses her to be in the highest place in Paradise—Jannah, Jannat al-Firdaus.

Jordan Salahuddin

Cousin

A Small Ball of Love and Warmth

I learned from Zamora to love and embrace life wholeheartedly—to never let a moment go to waste and to spread as much love as I can. Even when facing negativity, she taught me to find the positive and smile.

When I first saw Zamora after her leg amputation, the first thing she did was lunge at me for a hug. Despite the walker in her path, she stayed smiling and laughing. Just a small ball of love and warmth. She made people feel comfortable through her joy—by simply smiling and finding something to laugh about. I will strive to do the same: keep smiling.

Zamora left behind her constitution—her unwavering essence. She never let her battles change who she was, and she never allowed her resilience to waver. She remained strong, no matter the circumstance.

That has changed how I view life now. I realize that strength isn't always about pushing through aggressively—it's about holding onto your joy, your love, and your identity, even when life tries to take it from you.

Helping others and spreading love—that's one of the best ways I can continue to honor the light that Zamora brought into this world. Although I didn't spend as much time with her as I would have liked, she left a lasting impact on my heart.

In a world where adulthood can be overcomplicated, reflecting on Zamora's innocence and simplicity reminds me that she had the right approach: live with joy, give love freely, and stay true to yourself.

Thank you, Zamora.

Khalil Salim

Favorite Cousin

Showered with Love

I learned from Zamora that you can smile through some of the most difficult times in life. That even in darkness, we can be a light—for ourselves and for others. That we can be our best selves, even if we aren't in our best physical or mental condition. She taught me that the love we receive from family and friends can be used to power through obstacles some would say are impossible to overcome.

The greatest lesson I learned from my baby cousin is that the only one who knows what the future holds is our Creator. We should approach that future with positivity and love, because what we're going through is sometimes minuscule compared to the struggles of others—whether those people are in our lives or strangers we may never meet. And yet, those same people can still provide us with support, understanding, and love.

After finding out about her condition, every time I saw Zamora, she showed courage and strength. With her vibrant energy and intoxicating smile, you wouldn't even know there was anything going on. But the moment that truly cemented her strength and resolve for me was after her leg was amputated. We were at our grandma's house, and there she was—our beautiful princess—running around and playing with her cousins, using a walker, but with the same boundless energy she had as a little girl with both legs. Her smile had only grown bigger.

Every time I saw Zamora, I was showered with love. She would tell me I was her favorite cousin, and when we were together, she gave me no reason to doubt it. How could I not believe her? She never left my side when the family was together—whether we were watching something on the couch or cooking in the kitchen, she was always right there. And no matter how old or big she got, she always wanted me to pick her up and carry her. Doing so was a privilege—a memory I'll always treasure.

She was a beacon of curiosity, always asking questions about whatever we were doing or about my life. Whether it was work, a TV show, or a dish I was cooking, she wanted to know more. And I'm pretty sure that sometimes she asked just because I was the one doing it.

The way Zamora showed love was the purest kind. Her natural personality overflowed with affection. Just by being herself, she spread that love—an irresistible, radiant storm of happiness that touched everyone around her.

Zainab Salim

Aunt

Superhero

The most profound lesson I learned from Zamora was the importance of putting life's challenges into perspective. I came to understand that complaining is counterproductive; instead, I learned to appreciate and be more grateful for each experience—recognizing that even obstacles carry value and offer growth.

Whenever I need to summon the spirit of resilience, I reflect on Zamora—especially a moment during a family gathering before her major surgery to remove her right leg. While the rest of us grappled with the prognosis and the challenges ahead, Zamora saw only the possibilities. She reminded us that this change would make her more unique—perhaps even superhero-like. To her, the surgery wasn't a loss, but a gateway: a chance to live pain-free and regain mobility.

After the surgery, Zamora truly lived life like a superhero. She never hesitated to try new things or to continue the activities she loved—rock climbing, swimming, and especially dancing. In every step she took, she embodied Jet Li's wisdom: "Be like water." Her ability to adapt and thrive, even in the face of daunting circumstances, stands as a testament to her spirit, resilience, strength, and courage.

Zamora was always a loving young lady, greeting everyone with a bright smile and a warm embrace. But one of the things I will forever cherish about her was her incredible attention to detail. She had an eye for the little things that made being in her presence so special. I can still picture her noticing and admiring small changes—like a new hairstyle I tried or a fresh nail design I chose.

Because her love language made me feel so seen and appreciated, I now strive to pay it forward by being more mindful of how I make others feel in my presence.

Maryum Salim

Big Cousin

With Hardship Comes Ease

Be unapologetic, determined, and carefree. As the youngest grandchild, Zamora had so many cousins to look up to—and who looked out for her. Inevitably, she became someone we learned so much from. She didn't always say much, but she didn't have to. Zamora was radiant and demanded attention just by being herself.

In all our interactions, she was persistent about getting what she wanted—but always in a loving way. If you faced her with doubt or opposing intentions, she wouldn't let it shake her resolve. I loved that about her. Sometimes it got her into trouble with her parents, but her confidence was admirable.

Zamora embodied the saying: **"Sing like no one is listening, love like you've never been hurt, dance like nobody's watching, and live like it's heaven on earth."** The pureness of children is heartwarming. In Zamora's memory, I hope to channel my inner child and feel the bliss of being a kid again. She never let anyone or anything steal her joy, and I try to apply that to my own life.

I remember visiting Uncle Wali's house one summer and spending time with Zamora in her room. She was excited to see me and wanted me to play with all her toys. She showed me some art she made at school and handed me her favorite stuffed animal to hold. She demanded I play—without even needing to say a word—while she watched a video on her phone.

Suddenly, she was taken over by pain in her leg. She laid down and tried to fight through it. I could tell she didn't want me to be concerned or make a big deal about it. When I moved to get up and get help, she insisted I stay. She acted like she was okay. I told her it was okay to be in pain, but she still wanted us to keep playing.

It broke my heart to see her in pain. All she wanted to do was play and enjoy her time with me. She showed me resilience in real time, and I still think about that moment often. When I need to dig deep for strength in my own life, I think about Zamora—and all the different ways she showed strength over the years.

The Qur'an says, "Indeed, with hardship comes ease." (Qur'an 94:5) Through her joy and love, Zamora always made sure to grant herself ease.

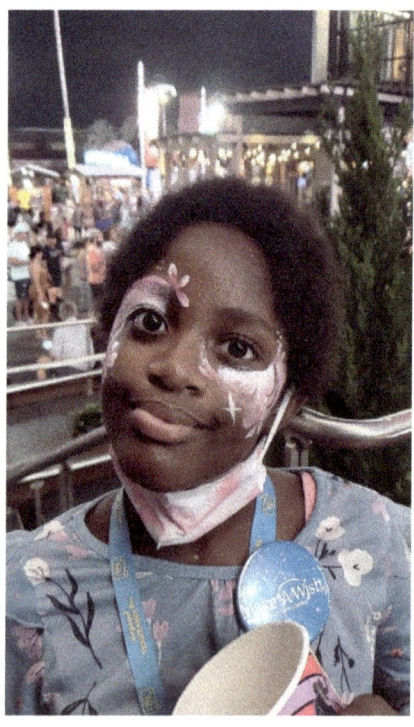

Georg Strasser

Lang Wiesen, Switzerland, Wali's Colleague

Positivity and Curiosity

I only knew Zamora through discussions with her father. Yet, through these conversations, she taught me the power of positivity and curiosity in the face of adversity. Her ability to seek joy in every moment was impressive and taught me to approach my own challenges with resilience, knowing that there is always something to look forward to, no matter the circumstances.

One of the most moving moments I learned about her was when she faced the amputation of her leg. Instead of fear, she expressed excitement about becoming "a robot." This outlook deeply impacted me, as it shows that sometimes it's not about traditional bravery, but rather about finding wonder in what is to come and embracing adventure.

As mentioned, I knew Zamora only through her father's eyes, but I always pictured her as someone with a beautiful way of making those around her feel special—whether through her infectious laughter or her singing to the beeping machines in the hospital. Living in the now and spreading love and kindness, even in small ways, is important.

Zamora's wise perspective on life and her ability to transform fear into joy have left a lasting impression on me—and on my wife as well, since we often talked about Zamora. She has taught us that life doesn't always have to be taken seriously and that finding joy in the moment is an important and powerful skill.

To honor Zamora's legacy, I want to embrace life with the same curiosity, positivity, and enthusiasm that she did. I also want to create joyful moments and adventures for others, just as her parents did for her.

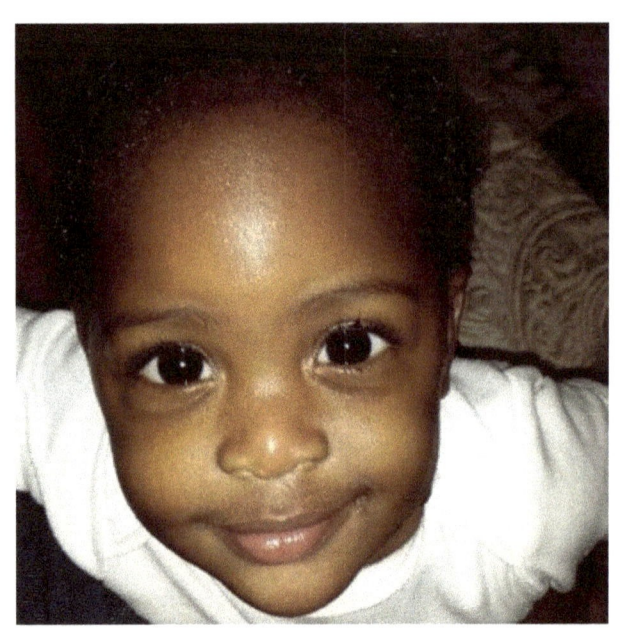

Definition of Terms

Osteosarcoma: A rare form of bone cancer that most commonly develops in the long bones of the arms and legs, particularly around the knee and shoulder areas. It primarily affects children and young adults, with peak incidence occurring during periods of rapid bone growth.

Port: A small medical device implanted under the skin, typically in the chest area, that provides easy access to veins for chemotherapy treatments, blood draws, and medication administration without repeated needle insertions.

Chemotherapy (Chemo): Treatment using powerful medications designed to destroy cancer cells or stop them from growing and dividing. These drugs are typically administered through an IV or port.

Fibula: The smaller of the two bones in the lower leg, running parallel to the tibia (shin bone).

Growth Plates: Areas of developing cartilage tissue near the ends of long bones in children and adolescents. When cancer "passes" the growth plates, it indicates the tumor has spread beyond its original location.

Nodules: Small, round masses of tissue that can be detected on medical scans. In cancer patients, these may indicate areas where the disease has spread.

Amputation: Surgical removal of a limb or part of a limb, sometimes necessary when cancer cannot be completely removed while preserving the affected body part.

Make-A-Wish Foundation: A nonprofit organization that grants wishes to children with critical illnesses, providing hope, strength, and joy during difficult times.

Camp Boggy Creek: A year-round camp in Florida that provides life-changing experiences for children with serious illnesses and their families, offering medical support alongside traditional camp activities.

Jumu'ah: The Friday congregational prayer that is central to Islamic practice, bringing the Muslim community together for worship and spiritual connection.

Masjid: An Islamic place of worship, also known as a mosque.

Salat: The Islamic practice of formal worship and prayer, performed five times daily.

Sujood: The act of prostration during Islamic prayer, where the forehead touches the ground in humble submission to Allah.

Alhamdulillah: An Arabic phrase meaning "Praise be to Allah," expressing gratitude and acknowledgment of God's blessings.

Rahimahullah: An Arabic phrase meaning "May Allah have mercy on her/him," typically said when remembering someone who has passed away.

Du'a: Personal prayer or supplication in Islam, where believers communicate directly with Allah.

Jannah/Jannat al-Firdaus: Paradise in Islamic belief; Jannat al-Firdaus refers to the highest level of Paradise.

Inna Lillahi wa inna ilayhi raji'un: An Arabic phrase meaning "Indeed, we belong to Allah, and indeed, to Him we shall return," commonly recited upon hearing news of someone's death, expressing acceptance of Allah's will and the temporary nature of life on Earth.

Definition for Osteosarcoma

Osteosarcoma is a type of cancerous bone tumor, specifically a malignant sarcoma, that arises from bone cells called osteoblasts. These cells are responsible for forming new bone tissue, but in osteosarcoma, the bone produced by these cells is not as strong or healthy as normal bone. It's the most common type of bone cancer, particularly in children, adolescents, and young adults.

Katie Williams-Johnson (Grandmother)
hanging with the kids at the Hollywood Parade

Danish Williams (Aunt)

98

Butterfly garden established as a memorial by Zamora's Elementary School (Nova Eisenhauser Elementary, Broward County Public Schools)

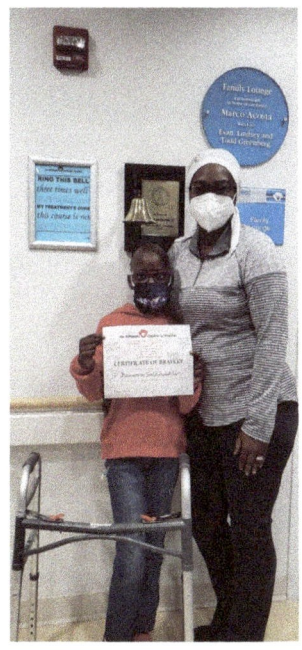

Zamora after completing chemotherapy (Feb. 2022)

Two of Zamaora's art pieces given to her cousin, Maryum

99

Princess Zamora during her Make-A-Wish Theme Park Experience

Princess Zamora meets Disney's Princess Tiana

Well equipped to swim in the Bahamas post amputation.

Horseback riding at Camp Boggy Creek

Zamora boating with Freedom Waters. She loved the water.

Zamora bowling at 3 years of age

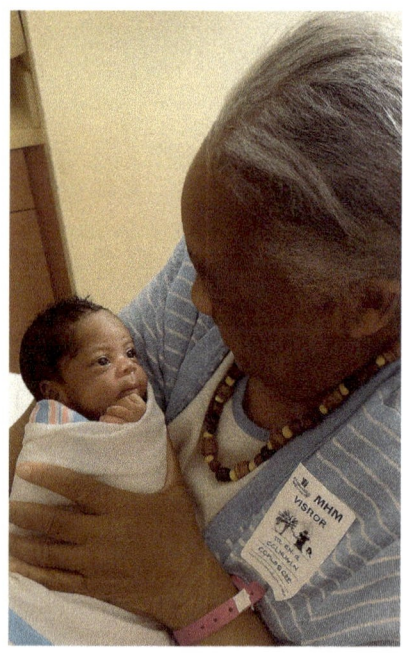

James Johnson (Grandfather)

*Grandmother visiting Zamora
in NICU*

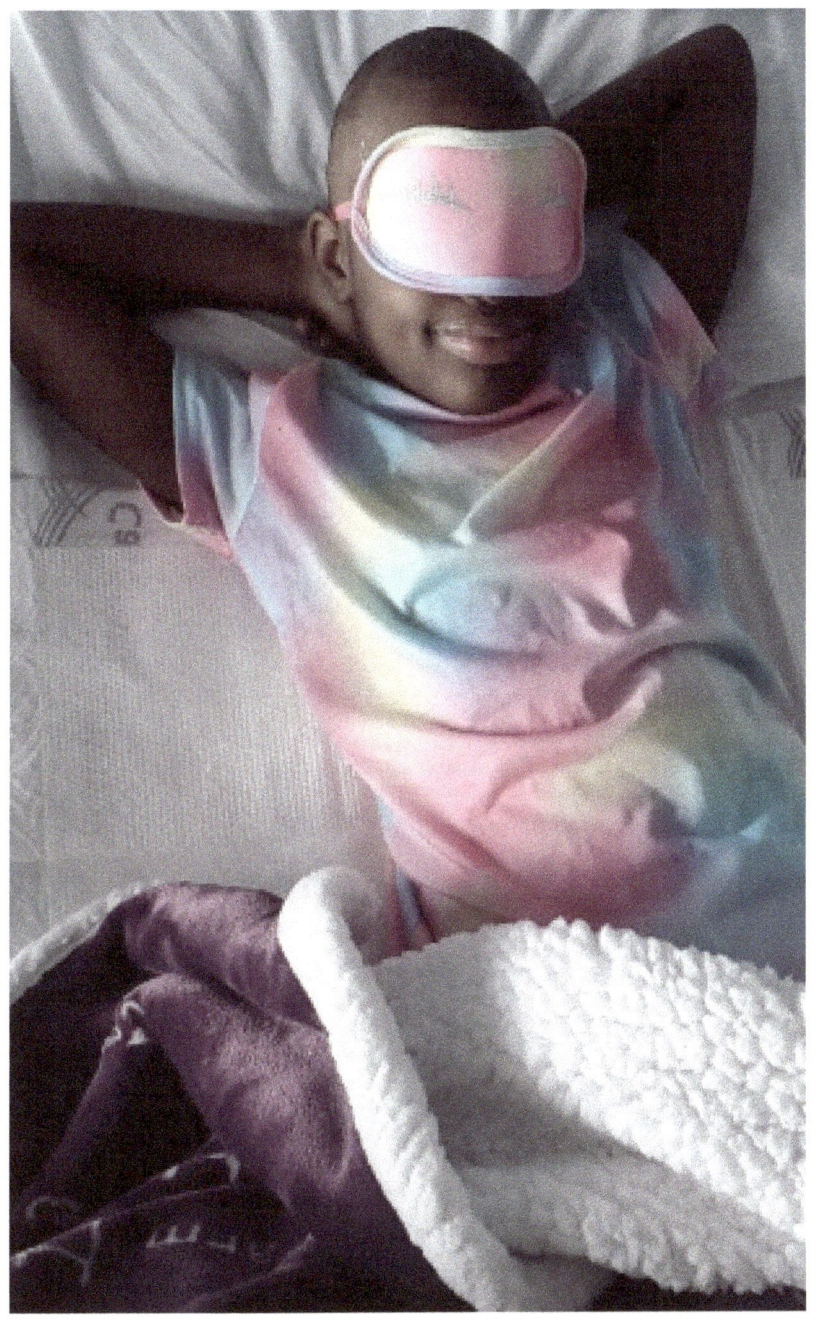

Zamora rocking her bald head like the queen she was. We bought wigs and hair accessories to prepare, but she wasn't having it. She loved her bald head and wore it proudly!

In loving memory of Zamora Salahuddin

November 18, 2013 – June 27, 2024
Princess Warrior Zamora

Her legacy of love, courage, and joy lives on in every heart she touched

I love how confident she is

and how she makes me laugh. Shes so awesome. Friend SHE'S

You are Positive You are You

- I like music
- I have curlie har
- I'm good in math
- I love Rink !
- I have one leg and I'm happy.

www.ingramcontent.com/pod-product-compliance
Lightning Source LLC
Chambersburg PA
CBHW051222120626
46547CB00013B/1472